PICTURES
and
PATTERNS

Words by Janet Margrie

Illustrations by Janet Seaward and Janet Margrie

RAINTREE CHILDRENS BOOKS
Milwaukee • Toronto • Melbourne • London

Copyright © 1977, Macdonald-Raintree, Inc.

Library of Congress Number: 77-8005

1 2 3 4 5 6 7 8 9 0 81 80 79 78 77

Printed and bound in the United States of America.

Library of Congress Cataloging in Publication Data

Margrie, Janet.
    Pictures and patterns.

    Includes index.
    SUMMARY: Easy-to-follow instructions for making
pictures and patterns in various media.
    1. Art — Technique — Juvenile literature.
[1. Art — Technique] I. Seaward, Janet.
II. Title.
N7433.M29 702'.8 77-8005
ISBN 0-8393-0117-0 lib. bdg.

Contents

Mixing Colors

1 Red, yellow, and blue are the primary colors. They cannot be made by mixing other colors.

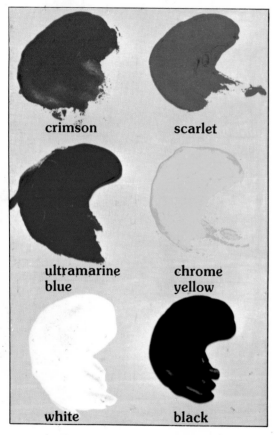

crimson

scarlet

ultramarine blue

chrome yellow

white

black

2 This is a good set of colors. It will make most other colors.

3 See how many colors you can make. First, paint big patches of crimson, scarlet, yellow, and blue.

4

4 Mix a tiny drop of another color with each of the first colors. Paint patches of the new colors.

5 Keep adding tiny drops to each color, making more and more colors.

5

Scribble Picture

This is not as easy as it looks. You will need paper and crayons or felt pens. Try doing a different kind of scribble for each part of the picture: zigzag, round and round, wavy, etc. Try scribbling two or three colors on top of each other.

7

Rubbings

You will need a piece of paper, crayons, and scraps of colored paper. You will also need scissors and glue.

Find some patterned surfaces which you can feel with the tips of your fingers. Lay a scrap of paper over the first surface. Hold the paper still (use tape if you need to). Rub over the paper with the side of your crayon. Do lots more rubbings. Cut them out and make up a picture or pattern with them. Glue them onto the paper.

9

Graph Paper Patterns

You can make many beautiful patterns by filling in the tiny squares of graph paper. Any paper with squares on it will do, but small squares are best. It is easiest to use felt pens or colored pencils for filling in.

Start by doing a simple pattern in one color. Repeat it a few times to make a larger pattern. Add another color, then add more and more until the pattern is finished. The same pattern will look very different if you do it again and change the colors. One pattern is shown four times on the opposite page, each time in different colors.

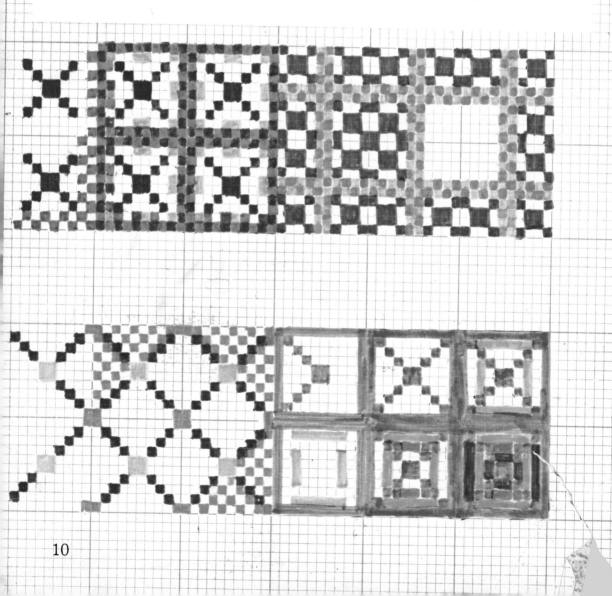

11

Picture in the Dark

You will need white paper, crayons, black writing ink, and a soft paintbrush. Draw a picture of something that happens in the dark. Press hard. Paint gently right over the whole picture with the ink. Now watch the picture glow out of the dark.

Strange Picture

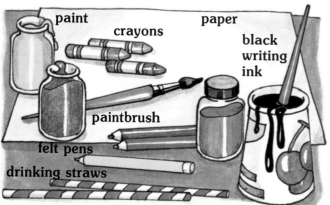

1 You will need these things.

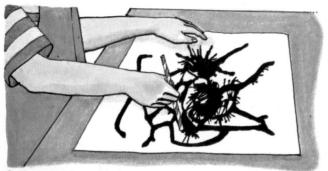

2 Drop a big blob of ink on the paper. Hold the straw close to the blot and blow. The ink will scatter all over the paper.

3 Drag the ink out with a straw to make spikes. When the ink is dry, turn your picture into something strange with your paints, felt pens or crayons.

Knife and Fork Picture

Try painting a picture without a brush. You could use blunt knives, forks, spoon handles or pieces of cardboard. Use thick paint.

If you mix some white glue with your paint first, your picture will look somewhat like an oil painting when it is dry.

Metal Plaque

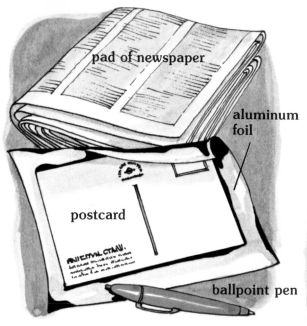

1 You will need these things.

pad of newspaper
aluminum foil
postcard
ballpoint pen

2 Lay the foil on the newspaper. Draw a picture with the pen.

3 Fill in the shapes with tiny patterns.

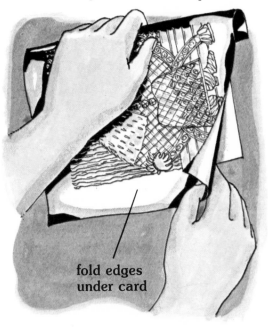

fold edges under card

4 Turn the foil over and cover the card with it.

18

19

Picture to Sew

Paint or crayon a picture on thin cardboard. Then, instead of drawing the fine lines, sew them with string or yarn. First prick holes with a pin. Tie a knot in one end of your string and glue or tape it to the back of the cardboard. Thread the other end through a darning needle. Sew through the holes you have made. You could do a crane, a fire engine or a sailing ship.

21

Glue Picture

You will need a tube or squeeze bottle of glue, a piece of thin cardboard and some newspaper.

Hold the glue upside down over the newspaper until it trickles out. Squeeze very gently — the glue may come out too fast. Practice trailing the glue onto the newspaper. Then trail your picture onto the cardboard. Leave it in a warm place to dry overnight.

When your picture is dry, you can paint it. Or you can take a print from it. The next page shows how.

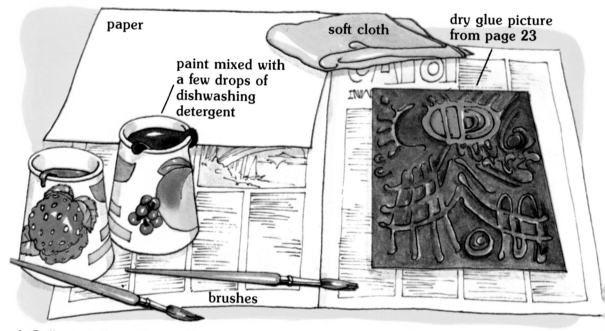

paper

paint mixed with
a few drops of
dishwashing
detergent

soft cloth

dry glue picture
from page 23

brushes

1 Collect all these things. Paint over your glue picture. Use paint
that is not too thick.

2 Lay the paper over the picture.
Rub gently with the cloth.

3 Lift the paper off. Now try
doing some more prints. They
will get better and better.

24

Big Easy Monoprint

You will need:

an old metal tray
paint, mixed with
    dishwashing detergent
some big sheets of paper

a big brush
a cloth
small pieces of thin cardboard
flat sticks

1 Clean the back of the tray and paint all over it.

2 Scrape a picture in the paint, using different scrapers.

3 Lay the paper on the paint. Smooth over it very gently.

4 Peek at each corner to see if print is ready. Then peel it off.

5 Look at your print. Was there too little paint or too much? Paint over the tray again. See if you can make a better print this time.

Cardboard Print

You will need:

two pieces of thin cardboard
scissors
a spoon
paint mixed with a little
    dishwashing detergent
a large paintbrush
paper

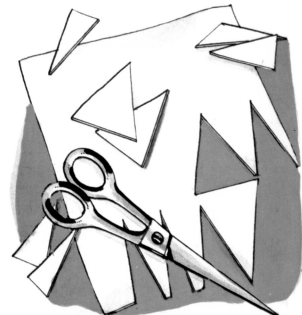

1 Cut some shapes from one piece of cardboard.

2 Paint over the other piece of cardboard. Quickly lay the shapes on it.

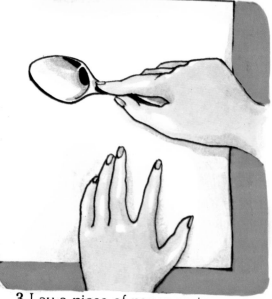

3 Lay a piece of paper on top. Rub all over the paper with the spoon. Do not let it slip.

4 Slowly peel off the paper.

Tissue Picture

colored tissue paper

white paper

white glue mixed with water

brush

scissors

1 You will need these things.

2 Cut or tear the tissue into shapes. Paint some glue onto the white paper. Place a piece of tissue on top.

3 Glue over the first piece of tissue. Place more pieces on top of it. Glue over it all again.

4 Add more layers of tissue and glue. Watch new colors appear as the pieces of tissue overlap.

31

Junk Collage

Collect some fairly flat junk like bottle tops or buttons. Arrange your junk on a piece of thin cardboard to make a picture or pattern. Use plenty of glue. When your picture is dry, put it under a heavy weight to flatten it.

Antique Panel

Lay a big piece of aluminum foil over your junk collage (see page 32). Press the foil down into the collage, starting with the deepest parts.

Fold the edges back. Brush over the foil with black shoe polish. When the polish has dried, rub lightly with a cloth.

Coming and Going Picture

1 Paint two very different pictures on pieces of thin cardboard.

2 Cut each picture into four pieces.

5 Pleat the picture like a fan. Spread it out a little.

Tape together behind.

3 Tape together the first piece from each picture.

4 Add a piece from each picture in turn until all the pieces are stuck together.

6 Stand your picture up. It will look different from each end.

Peep Show Picture

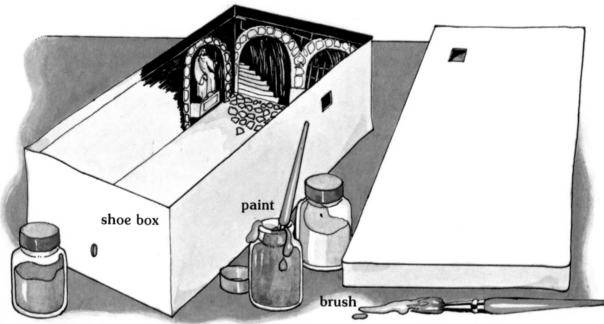

shoe box

paint

brush

1 You will need scissors, a flashlight, and all these other things. Cut a small hole in the end of the box. Cut a few more holes near the top.

2 Inside, make a picture of a dark place such as a cave or a secret tunnel. Shine the flashlight through each hole and see how the picture changes.

Story Picture

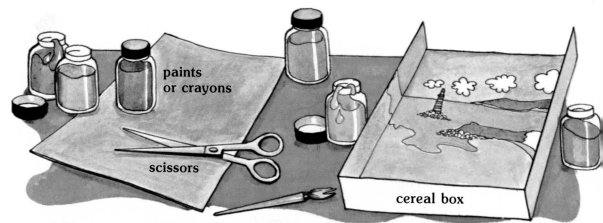

1 You will need these things. Cut the front off the box. Make a picture of a place you like inside the box.

2 Take the front of the box. On the plain side, draw the people and things you would like in your picture.

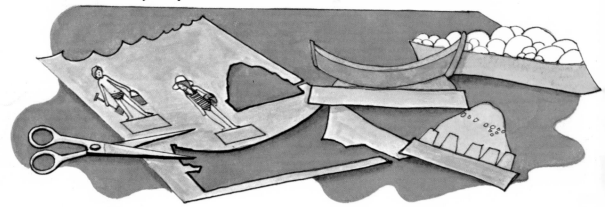

3 Draw a rectangle at the bottom of each picture to use as a stand.

4 Make up an exciting story and move the pieces as you tell it.

Things to Remember

While you work

Wear old clothes and cover yourself up. An apron or an old shirt buttoned at the back will keep you clean.

Collect all the things you will need. Clear a space to work and cover it with newspaper or a plastic cloth. Keep water away from your elbow and the edge of the table so you do not knock it over.

When you have finished, remember to wash the things you have used and put them away.

Brushes

It is best to have two brushes. Use a stiff one for mixing paint and laying it on thickly. Use a soft one for painting with watery paint or ink.

Paints

Poster paints and tempera paints give nice bright colors. Remember to put the lids back on tightly. You will need a large white plate or palette to mix paints. Solid discs of paint are good too. Put a large drop of clean water on each one while you get the other things ready. Mix your colors on the discs.

Water

Find a wide pot for your water so it cannot spill easily. A saucepan is good. If the pot is too small, the water will get dirty quickly and spoil your bright colors.

Paper

Try all kinds of paper. Shelf paper, newsprint, and wrapping paper are large and cheap. Construction paper comes in many colors and is good to paint on. Buy it in sheets or in a scrapbook. Shelf paper and writing paper are fine for making prints. Keep your spare paper away from the place you are working.

Drying prints

Before you begin to print, find a place to dry the wet prints. You can pin them to a board by one corner or make a clothesline between two chairs to pin your pictures on.

Glue

White glue, such as Elmer's School Glue, is all you need for the things in this book. Use it for gluing cardboard and for stirring into paint. Water it down a little when you glue tissue paper.

Keeping pictures flat

If your work curls up when it dries, put it under a heavy book overnight. Make sure the paint is really dry first.

Looking for Ideas

Visit your library, local museum or art gallery to see the pictures and patterns people have made in the past. They will give you some good ideas.

cave painting

Paintings on rocks in caves are the oldest ones we know. They often show the animals cave people hoped to catch when they went hunting. You could make pictures of things you want to happen.

Look at mosaics. They are pictures made of tiny pieces of stone and glass set in cement. You could make your own mosaic. Use small pieces of colored paper instead of stones. Glue the pieces onto paper.

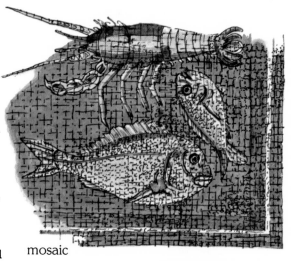
mosaic

If you visit an old mansion, you may see things that are both useful and beautiful, such as tapestries, embroidered chairs, and screens. Look at the unusual ways colors have been used together. Look for birds, dragons, and flowers. You may get some good ideas for your own pictures and patterns.

embroidery

part of a
sampler

Embroideries called *samplers* were once made by children to show how many different stitches they could sew. Try drawing or even sewing one yourself, making up the stitches as you go.

stained glass
window

Churches sometimes have stained glass windows. These are made from pieces of colored glass joined together with lead. See how the heavy black lines help to make the picture bolder. It is fun to make a window. Paint a picture with strong black lines on thin white paper. Then lightly coat the back of the paper with cooking oil. Hold it up to the light and the light will shine through it.

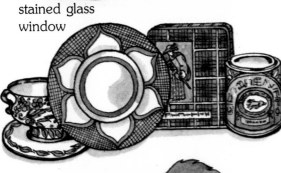

Search around the house for pictures and patterns. You will see them all around you in wallpapers, packages, clothes, and books. Look around outside for the patterns in nature. The bark of each tree has its own special pattern. The grain on a plank of wood can look like water. Clouds can make beautiful patterns in the sky. Open your eyes and see ideas everywhere.

Making Things with Pictures

You could make Christmas or birthday cards from your pictures. Make sure you have envelopes to fit them first.

strip of paper
to fit around book

Make a book cover with a picture on the front. The picture will stay clean longer if you varnish it.

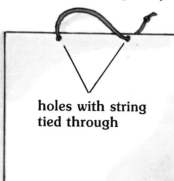

holes with string
tied through

paper strips glued
along edges

Try making picture frames from thin cardboard. Make holes near the top of the cardboard. Tie string through. Glue strips of paper along the edges. Glue your picture onto the cardboard.

Index

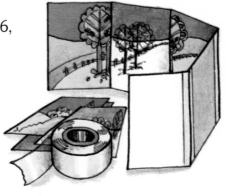